Deep i
Green Wood

a new collection of poems
by
Wes Magee

Illustrated
by
Celia Gentles

Caboodle Books

First published in Great Britain in 2012
by Caboodle Books Ltd

A Catalogue record for this book is available
from the British Library.

ISBN 978 0 9569482 6 7

Cover Illustration by Tom Truong
Inside Illustrations by Celia Gentles
Sketch of the author by Marianne Piano
Page Layout by Highlight Type Bureau Ltd
Printed by Cox and Wyman

Caboodle Books Ltd
Riversdale, 8 Rivock Avenue, Steeton, BD20 6SA
www.authorsabroad.com

Wes Magee
Deep in the Green Wood

Wes is an award-winning children's author
who has published more than 100 books
.....fiction, poetry, plays, picture books and anthologies.
A CD of his poems is available from 'The Poetry Archive'.
Wes travels around planet Earth
giving performances of his 'Poetry and Book Show'
and tutoring writing workshops.
He lives in Potter Brompton,
a tiny hamlet on the Yorkshire Wolds
where there are numerous green woods.
He has a dog (Maya – a golden retriever)
and dozens of goldfish.

Celia Gentles

Celia graduated at Wirral Metropolitan College, Birkenhead,
and now works as an artist,
illustrator.....and gardener!
She lives in a cosy caravan beside the sea.

Some of Wes Magee's Books

Poetry
Morning Break
The Witch's Brew
The Boneyard Rap
The Very Best of Wes Magee
The Phantom's Fang-tastic Show
So, you want to be a Wizard?

Fiction
The Scribblers of Scumbagg School
The Scumbagg School 'Scorpion'
Sports Day at Scumbagg School
The Spookspotters of Scumbagg School
The WinterWorld War
Blue, where are you?

Picture Books
The Legend of the Ragged Boy
Who likes Pancakes?
Stroke the Cat
The Emperor and the Nightingale

Plays
The Real Spirit of Christmas
The Working Children

Anthologies
The Puffin Book of Christmas Poems
Madtail Miniwhale
All Through the Day
A Shooting Star

Contents

Winter.....

People.....

Places.....

Start right here.....

Books are easy,
no plugs, cables,
or switches required.
>*You* are the power source,
>and your brain's
>fully wired.

So, switch off the TV,
hi-tech games,
and that mobile phone.
>This book's for reading,
>and it's for
>*you* alone.

Okay,
are you ready
to engage?
>Then start right here.
>It's easy.
>Just turn the page.....

Spooky .....

The Boneyard Rap

This is the rhythm
of the boneyard rap,
knuckle bones click
and hand bones clap,
finger bones flick
and thigh bones slap
when you're doing the rhythm
of the boneyard rap.
    Wooooooooooooooooo!

    It's the boneyard rap
    and it's a scare,
    give your bones a shake-up
    if you dare.
    Rattle your teeth
    and waggle your jaw,
    and let's do the boneyard rap
    once more.
        (.....eight finger snaps)

This is the rhythm
of the boneyard rap,
elbow bones clink
and backbones snap,
shoulder bones chink
and toe bones tap
when you're doing the rhythm
of the boneyard rap.
    Wooooooooooooooooo!

It's the boneyard rap
and it's a scare,
give your bones a shake-up
if you dare.
Rattle your teeth
and waggle your jaw,
and let's do the boneyard rap
once more.

> *(.....eight finger snaps)*

This is the rhythm
of the boneyard rap,
ankle bones sock
and arm bones flap,
pelvic bones knock
and knee bones zap
when you're doing the rhythm
of the boneyard rap.

> ***Wooooooooooooooooo!***

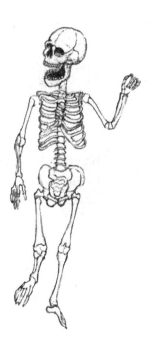

It's the boneyard rap
and it's a scare,
give your bones a shake-up
if you dare.
Rattle your teeth
and waggle your jaw,
and let's do the boneyard rap
once more.

> *(.....eight finger snaps)*

Yeah!

In the Castle of Gloom

Oh,
it's cold,
it's as cold as a tomb,
and
it's dark
as a windowless room,
in the Castle,
the Castle of Gloom.

(meet.....your.....doom)

No sun through the shutters.
No candle flame gutters.
No log embers glimmer.
No silver plates shimmer.
  No lamps in the hall.
  No brands on the wall.
  No moonbeams at night.
    No starshine.
    No light.

Oh,
it's cold,
it's as cold as a tomb,
and
it's dark
as a windowless room,
in the Castle,
the Castle of Gloom.

(meet.....your.....doooooooooom)

Wes Magee

City Sounds heard after Dark

The sweesh sweesh of speeding cars.
Old songs from the crowded bars.
Disco drums and loud guitars.

Aircraft zapping through the sky.
Rooftop cats that spit and cry.
Laughter from the passers-by.

Motorbikers' sudden roar.
Corner lads who josh and jaw.
A call. A shout. A slammed door.

The guard dogs that howl and bark.
Voices from the padlocked park.
City sounds heard after dark.

The Darkness

Oooh.....
the darkness.

We often find it scary,
yet the darkness is only there for a few hours
      while the Sun's away.
We *know* the Earth will spin on its axis
and the Sun return, as it always does,
      at dawn
      the next day.

Yet the darkness *can* be frightening.
For instance, when you're walking home after dark
      from a party, or a visit,
and suddenly you hear sounds behind you.
You look round, nervously. *"What was **that**?*
      What.....
      *what **is** it?"*

Perhaps it's nothing more
than footsteps, or a dog snuffling,
      or wind rustling leaves on the trees,
yet those sounds seem.....
so much *scarier* in the darkness.
      They can make you shiver.....
      or freeze.

And, after midnight,
you wake with a start
        when there's a sudden bang, or creak.
You lie in bed, stiff with fear,
although it's probably only a radiator cooling,
        or some bird tapping the window
        with its beak.

Really, there's nothing to fear about the darkness,
yet we're always relieved
        when the Sun returns to start a new day.
Then all those fears,
all those fears of the darkness,
simply vanish,
        simply vanish.....
        away.

But,
oooh.....
the darkness.

Exploring the Abandoned Mansion

In the hall.....
cobwebs hang from the crumbling ceiling,
antlered hat-stand's carved from oak,
crimson carpet's tattered and torn,
and dust in the air makes you choke.
    Chilly, icy mansion.
    Dank,
    abandoned
    place.

In the kitchen.....
tarnished taps drip brackish water,
stale loaf's grown a coat of mould,
a foul stench swims up from the drains,
and the radiators feel stone-cold.
    Fusty, foetid mansion.
    Damp,
    abandoned
    place.

On the landing.....
a headless, rusty suit of armour,
ancient portrait's green eyes glare,
cracked mirror in its silver frame,
and rat bones on the rocking chair.
    Echoing, creaky mansion.
    Dark,
    abandoned
    place.

In the bedroom.....
a tousled bed with blood-stained pillow,
rent drapes shiver in the breeze,
cockroach scuttles over floorboards,
and a sudden screech makes you freeze.
　　Faded, pallid mansion.
　　Dim,
　　abandoned
　　place.

In the attic.....
frayed dressing gowns have nests of mice,
there's Santa's sack for Christmas Eve,
a vampire bat hangs from a beam,
and the trap door's jammed when you try to leave.....
　　Creepy, scary mansion.
　　Dead,
　　abandoned
　　place.

Five Cemetery Epitaphs

1.
Here lies
Acker Abercrombie,
crazy name,
crazy zombie.
Slighty scary,
rather rude,
he walks at midnight
in the nude.

2.
Oh, two halves of Tracey Trump lie here.
She reached her eighty-seventh year.

She lived through floods and two World Wars.
Got sliced in automatic doors.

3.
Here resteth
Werewolf Walter Witz
who chewed relations
     into bits.
Aunts and uncles,
nephews, nieces,
all ended up
     Ripped **I**n **P**ieces.

4.

"Please mark my grave
      with just one flower."
That was the wish
of Cynthia Tower.
So when she died
they raised a plinth
and carved upon it
      'Hiya, Cynth!'

5.

Reserve this plot
   for Wes Magee,
convicted for
   bad poetree.
The judge declared
   his verse a crime,
and now poor Wes
   is doing
      rhyme.

The Ghosts of 'The Grange'

Miss Starvelling-Stamper died in 'twenty-four.
They found her stone-cold on the flagstone floor.

She lay beside the kitchen's cast-iron range,
last Starvelling-Stamper to dwell at 'The Grange'.

Since then the mansion's been abandoned, locked:
its windows smashed, roof collapsed, sewers blocked.

The croquet lawn's been lost to Queen Anne's Lace.
'The Grange' is now a sad, forgotten place.

Yet, nightly, ghosts creep from each crumbling wall
and gather in the leaf-strewn marble hall

- a chambermaid drifts up the wood-wormed stairs,
a skivvy flicks at cobwebs on the chairs,

two snooty butlers wait where moonbeams slant,
see there a grim and gaunt tiaraed aunt.

Miss Starvelling-Stamper's ghost – last of the line –
lifts to her lips a goblet of French wine

and floats above the kitchen's flagstone floor
where she was found stone-cold in 'twenty-four.

School.....

The Strangest School Secretary

She's Queen Wasp of the Office
and her throne's a swivel chair.
Her fingernails are purple.
A wren nests in her hair.

Her eyes are green as seaweed,
and she has a wildcat's stare.
She growls at timid teachers
just like a grizzly bear.

She makes Inspectors nervous
and drives the parents spare.
Headmaster, can't you sack her?
You're right: he'd never dare!

Our Secretary's the strangest.
She's really rather rare.
She's Queen Wasp of the Office
and her throne's a swivel chair.

teacher teacher

teacher teacher
you're the best
when you wear
that old string vest

        teacher teacher
        come here quick
        Stacey Brown's
        been *really* sick

teacher teacher
no more school
let's go down
the swimming pool

        teacher teacher
        I'm off home
        got to feed
        my garden gnome

Mr Grimm

Was he *born* old,
our teacher who always wore
that heavy, hairy, tweed jacket?
His bushy eyebrows would knit together
when he'd say weird things like,
"How old are you boy?"
    "Ten, Sir."
"Well, if you want to be eleven
finish those fractions, pronto! Compris?"
And he'd glare ferociously.

He had a habit
of always keeping his fists
stuffed deep in his trouser pockets,
and would violently shoulder his way
through the Staff Room door
rather than remove his hands.
We were convinced that Miss Protheroe,
our tired and timid Headmistress,
lived in mortal fear
of him.

Only once did we see him laugh;
that was when he caught
Judy Dutton giving John Staniforth
a big, wet, slobbery kiss
at the back of the classroom.
Mr Grimm growled,
"So, who are we then, Romeo and Juliet?"

and he gave an evil chuckle,
shoulders shaking,
chin pointing down into his tweed jacket.

At the Leavers' Concert in July
the eleven-year-olds did a surprise sketch
about the teachers.
Wayne Stubbs played Mr. Grimm,
with plastered-down hair,
stuck-on bushy eyebrows,
and fists stuffed deep into trouser pockets.
Wayne glared and growled grumpily.
We laughed and cheered.
Miss Protheroe squirmed in her chair.

Back in class Mr Grimm
stood staring out of the window, scowling.
After what seemed like an age
he muttered to himself,
"That Stubbs youth.....
he'll come to a sorry end, see if he doesn't."
Then he turned and glared at us,
eyebrows knitted together.
"Fractions!" he growled. *"Chop, chop! Fractions!"*
Normal service had been resumed.

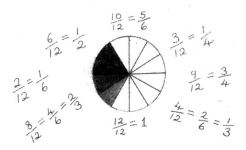

On the Playground

*The school playground, mid morning,
and there's
a deafening noise!
Three supervisors stand and watch
the screeching girls
and shouting boys.*

There's red light, green light, five stones,
and Who can capture the flag?
There's tig, there's tag, there's dodge ball,
there's elastics (in a snag).
There's stuck in the mud, skipping,
there's football, *and* running free.
So, what's the time, Mister Wolf?
A sailor went to sea sea sea.
There's British bulldog, leapfrog,
and there's Ready, Steady, Go!
There's hopscotch, kiss chase, frog jump,
chants of *eee i aady oh.*
Mr Crocodile, may I
cross the golden river, *please?*
There's marbles, jacks, there's wall ball,
there's eight, nine, ten.....and all freeze!
Now the farmer's in his den,
and there's standing on your head.
Horses, hopping, hide and seek,
and handstands, *and* acting dead.

Wes Magee

A line follows the leader,
netball (so, *who's* keeping score?),
there's one potato, two potato, three potato four.
The litter bin's a wicket,
sweatshirts make posts for the goal.
There's sardines, sevens, I spy,
there's line kicks, *and* rock 'n' roll.

> *Then the bell rings.*
> *Silence falls,*
> *and mid morning playtime ends.*
> *The pupils troop back into the school,*
> *friends with*
> > *friends with*
> > > *friends.*

No Homework Tonight, *Please*

Why?
Because I've been doing
school work all day long,
and this evening I just want to
run, race, shout, sneeze,
rest, roll, find, freeze,
screech, scream, mess, mime,
dance, dig, rap, rhyme
and, of course, climb.
    So,
       no homework tonight,
       please.

When
I get home
there's just so, so much
for me to do. I just want to
explore, eat, trick, talk,
bend, bounce, watch, walk,
push, pick, laugh, leap,
lounge, laze, catch, creep
and, of course, sleep.
    So,
       no homework tonight,
       please.

Down by the School Gate

There goes the bell,
it's half past three
and down by the school gate
you will see......

> **Ten** mums talk talk talking,
> **Nine** babies squawk squawking,
> **Eight** toddlers all squabbling,
> **Seven** grans on bikes, wobbling.....

> **Six** dogs bark, bark, barking,
> **Five** cars stopping, parking,
> **Four** child-minders running,
> **Three** bus drivers sunning.....

> **Two** teenagers dating,
> **One** lollipop man waiting.....

The school is out,
it's half past three
and the first to the school gate
is......*me*!

Summer Holidays, Approaching

For weeks, *weeks,*
I've waited for this moment
when the school year is about to end
and the summer holidays begin.

In our classroom
the wall displays of art work
have been torn down,
tables tidied,

pens, pencils, rulers collected in,
worksheets put away,
reading books stowed on shelves,
and the computers switched off.

By the door
there's a heap of plastic sacks
crammed with rubbish,
ready for the caretaker to cart away.

The SMART Board is blank.
The classroom seems so bare,
so.....*so* empty,
and our voices echo strangely.

Weeks ago it seemed
this moment would never arrive
but now it's almost here.
Only minutes, *minutes* to go.

Teacher stands at her desk,
arms folded. She looks really tired.
The Head pokes his bald head
round the door.

*"Enjoy the holiday, everyone.
Care on the roads. Be helpful at home."*
It's his usual speech.
We've heard it all before.

Suddenly there's shouting in the corridor.
A class is out early!
But now *we're* stacking chairs on tables,
and rushing towards the door.

Teacher's last words are drowned
in the growing din.
Everyone's shoving
and talking, gabbling excitedly.

The cloakroom heaves with bodies
as we grab gear, haul on backpacks,
and noisily barge and bang our way out
through the swing doors.

"See you!" we call
across the playground,
then go our separate ways.
The last pupil swings on the school gate.

Yes, this is the moment I've waited weeks for,
weeks,
and now it's here:
the holidays, *at last!*

I head for home,
the sun's beaming down,
and the long summer, the *looooooong* summer,
stretches before me.....

the holidays
AT LAST!

Wes Magee

Sea.....

Beach Quest

So, what did we see
at Runswick Bay
as we walked the beach
on that hot summer's day?

Smooth, round pebbles, and a seagull's bones,
a weathered tree trunk, starfish and stones,
bleached driftwood, and a tangled old net,
tiny pieces of shiny black jet,
ammonite fossils in the cliff face,
coloured seashells, a crab's carapace,
coils of thick rope - all knotted and frayed,
and shallow pools through which we could wade.

Long stalks of seaweed, bendy as whips,
taste of salt water on our dry lips,
a wild, chasing dog, barking like mad,
toddlers throwing wet sand at their dad,
green glass glinting in bright summer sun,
jellyfish - counted one hundred and one,
paddling in waves, right up to our knees,
and a liner far out on the high seas.

Yes, that's what we saw
at Runswick Bay
as we walked the beach
on that hot summer's day.

Merman and Mermaid

Merman:	It's King Neptune's birthday, and his party's today. It's at Coral Palace which is far, far away.
Mermaid:	How.....how far?
Merman:	Oh, beyond Atlantis where the sea serpents lurk and long eels are twisting in the mud and the murk.
Mermaid:	But first, I must.....
Merman:	We'll make the long trip on the back of a whale. If you start to slide off just grab hold of its tail.
Mermaid:	.....comb my golden locks!
Merman:	Well, all right, hurry up. There's no time to delay. King Neptune awaits us and his party's today.

Flashing Light......Far Out at Sea

It was late,
  growing dusk,
    when we headed back to the car
      after our long, long day
        on the beach.

      There we were,
        a straggle of family and friends
        carting rugs, picnic hamper,
      fold-up seats, frisbees,
    spades, bats and balls.

It seemed such a long trek
  to the car park,
    and it was almost dark
      when someone shouted,
        "See that?"

      We stopped,
        and after a minute
      there it was:
    a single flash of light..... far out at sea.
"See it? See that?"

Another minute passed
  and the light flashed again.
    "What is it?"
      Lighthouse? Lightship? What?
      No one knew.

Laden with beach gear
we struggled up
the massive sand dunes.
Now it was really dark.
"Look! There it is again!"

We stopped at the top
to catch our breath,
and watched as the light flashed,
before plodding on
to the car park.

We did so much
that long, long day at the beach
but what I remember most
was that light flashing
.....far out at sea.

That strange light,
soundless,
mysterious,
flashing.....
flashing.....
flashing.....

Humpback Whale

Our living island,
your sad song echoes
beneath the icebergs.

Survive and swim free
in the cold oceans,
our living island.

Sea.....Creatures

Dolphins.....leapers,
   king crabs.....creepers,
     starfish.....clingers,
       stingrays.....stingers,
         sharks.....attackers,
           swordfish.....hackers,
             salmon.....swimmers,
               flying fish.....skimmers,
             great whites.....biters,
           anglerfish.....lighters,
         spoon worms.....slitherers,
       shrimps.....ditherers,
     lobsters.....snappers,
   electric eels.....zappers,
barracudas.....stalkers,
   mudskippers.....walkers,
     tiger sharks....robbers,
       seahorses.....bobbers,
         bouncing fish.....bouncers,
           sea anemones.....pouncers,
           blue whales.....gushers,
             octopi.....crushers,
               giant squid.....reachers,
               see.....sea creatures.

What the Divers Found.....

To the east of Crooked Island
   in the blue Caribbean Sea
divers located a pirates' sloop
   that went down in '93.

They discovered broken cutlasses,
   rusted anchor, precious stones,
a thousand scattered silver coins,
   and the pirates' whitened bones.

They came across tattered sailcloth,
   doubloons, daggers, a drum,
slime-coated barrels of brandy,
   and flagons of Indies rum.

They saw the ship's wheel - encrusted.
   Espied a huge hole in the hull.
Found musket shot, a grappling hook,
   and the captain's fractured skull.

They spotted a worm-eaten peg leg,
    cracked compass, a lash and a whip,
a map tightly wrapped in an oilskin
    which they took back to their ship.

Yes, the divers brought back their booty,
    yet none of them, *none* of them knew
where that wrecked sloop was headed
    or could name the piratical crew.

There's a mystery here, a strange secret:
    there's a tale that needs to be told,
of treachery, treason, and terror,
    of treasure maps and gold,

and why that sloop and its pirates
    in the year 1693
went down east of Crooked Island
    in the blue Caribbean Sea.

The Red Boat

There goes the Sun
  slowly sailing by,
    like a red boat
      on the ocean of the sky.

There goes the Sun
  all the day through,
    a red boat sailing
      across its sea of blue.

Wes Magee

Space.....

What is......the Sun?

The Sun is an orange dinghy
    sailing across a calm sea.

It is a gold coin
    dropped down the drain in Heaven.

The Sun is a yellow beach ball
    kicked high into the summer sky.

It is a red thumbprint
    on a sheet of pale blue paper.

The Sun is a milk bottle's gold top
    floating in a puddle.

The Howler of the Purple Planet

Far beyond our Solar System,
where exists no ray of light,
spins the fog-wrapped Purple Planet
      in an endless night.

Space Police when passing Purple –
on the watch for Killer Zeds,
heard a fearsome, ice-cold howling
      deep inside their heads.

Men have never been to Purple,
never flown down through its fog.
Was the howling caused by gales,
      or by a mutant dog?

As the spaceship hurtled onward,
leaving Purple far behind,
so the howling echoed madly
      through each spaceman's mind.

One man's blood was turned to water:
three more were quite soon to die,
all because they'd heard that ghostly,
      disembodied cry.

Far beyond our Solar System,
where exists no ray of light,
spins the fog-wrapped Purple Planet
      in an endless night.

The ZZZ

The treble Z from Planet Zell
  is the first hi-techno creature.
    She's powered by atomic waste,
      and at top speed she's a *screecher.*

      Transistors crackle in her ears,
    hot re-entry makes her blister.
  But if you think she's ugly, well,
you should *see* her sister.

On data input Z is fed
  and she's cooled by a thermostat.
    Her fingers shoot red laser beams:
    across Zell she streaks with a

              SPLAT!

The Blob

"And......what is it like?"
> "Oh, it's scary and fat-bumped
> and spike-eared and groany.
> It's hairy and face-splumped,
> and its bottom's all bony."

"And......where does it live?"
> "Oh, in comets and space probes
> and pulsars and blackholes.
> In craters and caverns,
> and icy-cold northpoles."

"And......what does it eat?"
> "Oh, red rocks and fishlegs
> and x-rays and mooncrust.
> Then lava and sun-eggs
> all sprinkled with spacedust."

"And......who are its enemies?"
> "Oh, Zonkers and Moonquarks
> and Sunspots and Bigbags.
> Dumb Duncers and Smogsters
> and zip-zapping Zigzags."

"And......and......what does it wear?"

> "Not a thing.

> It's *bare.*"

On Charlotte's Bedroom Ceiling

During daytime
there's little to see
on Charlotte's
bedroom ceiling,

but at night,
when the light's switched off,
you'll see something strange
and revealing.

In the darkness,
stars, planets and moons
glow luminously.
It's really *most* appealing.

Comets and meteorites zoom,
and spiral galaxies
are silently turning
and wheeling.

At night, gaze up
and you can see the universe
on Charlotte's
bedroom ceiling.

My Place in Space

I
live
at
Comet Cottage,
Star Street,
Venus Village,
near Moonchester,
Plutoland,
Great Britain,
Europe,
Northern Hemisphere,
Planet Earth,
the Solar System,
Orion-Cygnus Arm
of the Milky Way Galaxy,
the Universe,
Infinity

and
beyond

.

.

.

One Day?

One day
we'll land on planet Mars.

One day
we'll travel to the stars.

One day
we'll live upon the Moon.

This year?

Next year?

One day?

Soon?

Deep in the Green Wood.....

Deep in the Green Wood

"Here in my cottage
deep in the green wood
I live on my own
and I eat children pud.
No one would guess
that I'm up to no good
here in my cottage
deep in the green wood.

"I stand at the door
and I look very nice.
My lipstick is red
and my eyes green as ice,
and my cottage is made
of sugar and spice
with caramel cats
and marzipan mice.

"Children lost in the wood
stop off here to eat.
My windows and walls
they find such a treat.
They think that I'm great
and terribly sweet
when I ask them inside
to rest their tired feet.

"As soon as they're trapped
I bolt the front door.
The shocked kids see bones
all over the floor.

They see I'm a witch
with warts on my jaw,
one broken brown tooth
and a wig made of straw.

"The kids try to hide
in my smelly old room
but I soon sniff them out
in the cobwebby gloom.
I give them a whack
with a dirty great broom
and into my oven
they go to their doom.

"I bake the lost kids
till they're tender and nice,
then serve them up hot
with lashings of rice.
I garnish with gnats
and finely-ground lice
here in my cottage
of – *hah!* – sugar and spice.

"Their parents come searching,
just as they should,
but none of them guess
that I'm up to no good,
or that their lost kids
are yum scrummy pud,
here in my cottage
deep in the green wood."

The Witch's Brew

Hubble Bubble at the Double,
cooking pot stir up some Trouble!

Into my pot
there now must go,
a leg of lamb
and green frog's toe.
Old men's socks
and dirty jeans,
a rotten egg,
and cold baked beans.

Hubble Bubble at the Double,
cooking pot stir up some Trouble!

One dead fly
and a wild wasp's sting,
the eye of a sheep
and the heart of a King.
A stolen jewel
and mouldy salt,
then for good flavour
a jar of malt.

Hubble Bubble at the Double,
cooking pot stir up some Trouble!

Wing of bird
and head of mouse.
Screams and howls
from 'The Haunted House'.
And don't forget
the jug of blood,
or the sardine tin,
or the clod of mud.

Hubble Bubble at the Double.
cooking pot stir up
SOME
TROUBLE!

The Cross Country Race
through Wolds Wood

10 lost their way in the back of beyond.

9 slipped in mud and fell into a pond.

8 snagged their shorts on some rusty barbed wire.

7 tried, but failed, to light a camp fire.

6 were pursued by a mad-barking dog.

5 grazed their knees when they slipped off a log.

4 played at War and their leader was Mick.

3 gobbled chestnuts until they were sick.

2 fell asleep on a huge mossy stone

and **1** lost her knickers and ran back alone.

Now.....
can you work out in your massive brain space
how many started the cross country race?

(Answer on page 112)

Collecting Conkers

Hey,
collecting conkers
in the
autumn.

Beneath tall chestnut trees
I sought
'em.

When some fell fast
I deftly caught
'em.

Back to our shed
I did transport
'em.

Now on a
wooden bench I sort
'em.

Hey,
collecting conkers
in the
autumn.

The Old Tree Stump

The old tree stump
is all that remains
of an elm tree
felled years ago.
Now it's our garden seat
comfortably covered
with a moss cushion
upon which our cat
sleeps in the sun.

A dead stump?
Peel back the bark
and see scores of ants
swarming like Londoners
in the rush hour,
or watch the woodlice
trundling like army tanks
to the front line
of some forgotten war.

And, look, here's a centipede
plunging down a crack
like a potholer
exploring unknown caverns.
Later, when we've gone,
a thrush alights
and uses the stump as an anvil
upon which to smash
a land snail's shell.

It's a favourite spot
in our garden,
this old tree stump
and - you know -
it's quite the best
place to sit
and sun yourself
on a sweltering day
in the middle of July.

The Cyclists' Adventure

One summer Sunday we biked to Dore Wood,
me, the red-haired Pike brothers, and Dave Hood.

We sped along dirt tracks dappled in shade,
and dumped our bikes in a grassy-green glade

where we built a den with sticks. Our shouts rang
until six youths came, smoking: a tough gang.

Hearts thumping we fled like four startled deer
but then, when we were almost in the clear,

my bike crashed! I was thrown, and banged my head.
Dazed, I lay in long grass wishing I was dead.

The gang yanked me up, swore, blew rings of smoke,
and then they let my tyres down for a joke.

How they laughed. One youth Chinese-burned my wrist.
Another held a sharp knife in his fist.

Surrounded there, I brushed aside my tears,
and as I did I wiped away my fears,

for as they joshed my anger grew and grew
and then I spoke the harshest words I knew.

My verbal fireworks gave them cause to frown.
They looked confused. I saw their mouths turn down.

Bewildered by my endless ranting flow
they pumped deflated tyres.......and let me go!

And as I raced along the earthy track
the gang's half-hearted jeers bounced off my back.

Soon I had reached the far edge of Dore Wood
and found the red-haired Pike boys and Dave Hood.

"What happened?" "Tell us!" "How'd you get away?"
I grinned, and said, *"No sweat.* **Words** *won the day!"*

*　　*　　*　　*

Years on, I still recall that Sunday when
I went with pals to build a woodland den,

and saw off gang of bullies – *timid birds!* –
by letting loose the punching power of words.

In Bluebell Wood

In Bluebell Wood
on a bright May day
   see
white butterflies flutter,
brown rabbits scutter,
black beetles creep,
and fawn deer leap.
   Watch
green frogs splash,
red fox cubs dash
as the orange sun winks
and a grey owl blinks.
   Now
pink blossom falls,
an olive cuckoo calls,
beige sparrows play
and blue bluebells sway,
   and sway,
   and sway,
   and sway,
   and sway
in Bluebell Wood
on a bright May day.

The Woodland Haiku

Fox
Slinks to the wood's edge
and – with one paw raised –
surveys the open meadows.

Fallow Deer
Moves as smooth as smoke
and starts at an air tremor.
Is gone like a ghost.

Rabbits
Blind panic sets in
and they're off: dodgem cars
way out of control.

Rooks
They float high above,
black as scraps of charred paper
drifting from a fire.

Owl
Blip on his radar
sends owl whooshing through the dark,
homing in on mice, rats.

Pike
Killer submarine
she lurks deep in the woodland's
green-skinned pond. Lurks......waits.

Sheep's skull
Whitened and toothless,
discovered in a damp ditch.
A trophy for home.

Humans
Clumsy, twig-snapping,
they see nothing but trees, trees.
The creatures hide......watch......

Love.....

I like Emma

I like Emma
but I don't know
if she likes me.
All the boys
think I'm a
fool.

I wait
beside the school gate
at half past three
trying to keep my cool.
Emma walks past,
shaking her long hair free,
laughs with her friends
and drifts off home
for tea.

Emma's two years older
than me.
Her class is higher
up the school.

I like Emma
but I don't know
if she likes me.
All the boys
think I'm a
fool.

First Love

I love Hazel
but she doesn't know it.
How do I tell her?
How do I show it?

As usual, we leave school together,
but today has an extra special glow
for - *Yes!* - it's the start of the Christmas break.
In freezing cold December dusk we make
our way home. As we walk it starts to snow.
Hazel, excited, says, *"Christmas weather!"*

She stops when we reach the darkened old church
and says, *"Bet you daren't walk through there alone!"*
She points to the spooky graveyard..... so dark.
In summer we'd take this short cut for a lark,
but now..... in winter darkness..... on my own?
"Easy," I boast, but my heart gives a lurch.

I love Hazel,
but she doesn't know it.
How do I tell her?
How do I show it?

Hazel says, *"Meet me on the other side.
Go on, Wes!"* She laughs and touches my arm.
I gulp, and push back the wrought iron gate
wondering if I'll meet some dreadful fate,
then tread the flagstone path and - *in alarm!* -
hear a stifled cry. I quicken my stride,

pass lichened headstones that seem set to fall
and yew trees rustling in the chill wind's moan.
I run towards the locked church, round the tower,
and race on as a clock chimes the half-hour.
Spooked, I shiver, then reach the safety zone -
the exit lych-gate. Now I'm walking tall!

I love Hazel
but she doesn't know it.
How do I tell her?
How do I show it?

I'm back on the snowy street, breathing hard,
while inside my chest my heart thumps and lifts.
I lean against a lamppost, bathed in light,
and wait for Hazel. Now she comes in sight,
her backpack bulging with books, cards and gifts.
"Wes, you made it!" she calls. *"How was the graveyard?"*

"No prob," I croak. *"You.....were my lucky charm."*
Hazel steps up, takes my hand in her glove
and plants an oh-so-soft kiss on my cheek.
Spotlit beneath the streetlight I go weak
at the knees. The Christmas hols..... and I'm in love!
As snow falls we head for home..... arm in arm!

> I love Hazel
> and now she knows it.
> Together we walk,
> together we show it.

> Oh, *how* we show it!

Our Miss Gill and Mr. Scott

Our Miss Gill
and Mr. Scott
do seem
to like each other
rather a
lot.

His class
and our class
are always going on trips
together,
and today we climbed
Tucker's Hill
in *dreadful* weather.
  "He held her hand."
  "Never!"
  *"He did. **And** they kissed."*
  "No!"
It turned terribly cold.
  "I'm freezing!"
 said
Jill.

It started to rain,
then there was sleet,
and then
there was
snow.

At least it was warm on the coach
and we all sang.
Arrived back
at the school gate
just
as the hometime bell
rang.

Off we trooped,
but at the street corner
I turned
and looked back.
And so did
Jill.

We watched
as our Miss Gill
and Mr. Scott
crossed the car park
hand in glove.
   *"They **are** in love,"*
said
Jill.

Yes,
they do seem
to like each other
rather a
lot.

Uncle Stan and Aunt Sue

They looked down, smiling,
as you lay in your cot,
uncle Stan with his whiskers,
shiny bald head, and loud laugh,
and aunt Sue in her silky dress
and smelling sweetly of lavender.

Every birthday you received their card
with its neat handwriting in blue ink,
and a carefully folded new £5 note inside.
They were characters, real characters,
who lived life to the full
and were often talked about in your family.

Once, uncle Stan, on some madcap adventure,
got lost in the Amazon rainforest
and ended-up in hospital for six months.
Then, on a Caribbean cruise,
aunt Sue fell overboard, nearly drowned,
and had to be rescued by a motor launch.

When uncle Stan retired, they went to live
in a small bungalow on the Isle of Wight.
It was too, too far away to visit
so you didn't see them for years, years,
yet annually their birthday card to you arrived
with the carefully folded new £5 note inside.

In time they grew old, and you noticed
how the neat handwriting in blue ink was shakier.
All your life, it seemed, they were there for you,
like rocks of certainty in a changing world,
and I guess you thought they'd go on for ever.
But, in time, you received news of their deaths.

Twice you crossed by hovercraft to the island
to attend their funerals
and said your sorrowful goodbyes.
It was just so, so sad
to know they were gone
and that you'd never see them again.

You'll never forget uncle Stan with his whiskers,
shiny bald head and loud laugh,
or aunt Sue in her silky dress
and smelling sweetly of lavender.
What great characters they were,
and they'd always been there for you. But no more.

Of course, you've kept all the birthday cards
with their neat handwriting in blue ink,
treasured mementoes, but now
uncle Stan and aunt Sue are gone, gone for ever,
and you feel..... an emptiness.
It's just, well, so sad.

It's so sad.

Caitlin, or Cherie, or Claire?

It's a scorching Friday in July
as pupils spill from the school at lunchtime
and spread far across the field under a sweltering sun.

With legs splayed three girls sit on the grass
and pick oxeye daisies by the score.
Chanting, they pluck the white petals one by one......

> *"He loves me,*
> *he loves me not,*
> *he loves me,*
> *he loves me not....."*

From a flawless blue sky the sun glares down,
its eye unblinking. Plucked petals lie,
curling, curling in the heat-stunned air.

The girls chant lazily, dreamily wondering
who'll be the one to get lucky with Richard.
Will it be Caitlin, or Cherie, or Claire?

> *"He loves me,*
> *he loves me not,*
> *he loves me,*
> *he loves me not....."*

Family.....

Who?

"Who," asked my mother,
"helped themselves to the new loaf?"
  My two friends and I
  looked at her
  and shrugged.

"Who," questioned my mother,
"broke off the crust?"
  Three pairs of eyes
  stared at the loaf
  lying on the kitchen table.

"Who," demanded my mother,
"ate the bread?"
  No one replied.
  You could hear
  the kitchen clock.
  Tick. Tock.

  And
even today I can taste it,
crisp, fresh, warm from the bakery,
and I'd eat it again
if I could find a loaf
like that,
   mmmmm,
   like *that*......

Wes Magee

My Dog's First Poem

(to be read in a dog's voice)

My barking drives them
up the wall.
I chew the carpet
in the hall.
I love to chase
a bouncing ....*banana?*

Everywhere I leave
long hairs.
I fight the cushions
on the chairs.
Just watch me race
right up the ....*shower?*

Once I chewed
a stick of chalk.
I get bored when
the family talk.
Then someone takes me
for a ....*wheelbarrow?*

The Family's Game of Cricket

A summer's day
and the family's here
for a game of cricket.
I stab three sticks
in our back lawn
for the wicket.

A twig for bails.
My new tennis ball.
And, *hey*, what a dream team!
There's me, my big sister, grandma,
dad, uncle Jock, aunt Maisie,
and our cat, Cream.

But then, apart from me,
no one knows how to play!
They can't bat, or bowl, or catch.
Or keep wicket. Useless!
And now, oh just great, here comes our wild dog,
Patch.

In a flash the ball's in his teeth
and he's off like the wind.
That dog is..... completely mad!
We give chase: that's me, my big sister,
grandma, uncle Jock, aunt Maisie,
Cream the cat..... and dad.

Yes, you've guessed it!
Mum arrives (in her high heels, no less)

carrying a tray laden with drinks and cake.
Patch crashes into her legs.
Down goes mum.
Lemonade spreading..... like a..... like a lake!

The family's game of cricket?
Hah, you can forget it.
It was hopeless. *And* my new tennis ball's gone.
And what did uncle Jock say, stupidly?
"Whose for tiddlywinks?
Anyone?"

> ### *Grrrrrrrr!*
> (and that's me,
> not Patch!)

The Spoons Music Man

My Uncle
made music with spoons.

He could play
any number of tunes.

He banged them
on knees and his nose.

He banged them
on elbows and toes.

My Uncle
made wonderful tunes.

He made
magical music with spoons.

The Family Clan

There we were.
Oh, what a crowd,
the family clan,
and so, *so* loud!
Shouty and screechy
and yakky and gabby,
and
all gobbling lunch
at Fountains Abbey.

There was uncle Sam from Birmingham,
auntie Bess from near Loch Ness,
cousin George from Cheddar Gorge,
and grandad Brown from Swindon Town.
There was gran McGork from County Cork,
nana Spear from Blackpool pier,
grandpa Fred from Beachy Head,
and nephew Brent from Stoke-on-Trent.
There was Patch (our dog) from Baxter's Bog,
niece Lou-Ann from the Isle of Man,
cousin Dean from Turnham Green,
and Patrick's boys (*they* made noise!).
There was brother Jole from Wookey Hole,
sister Fran from Kurdistan,
great-grandma Lill from Pentonville,
and uncle Lee from the sands of Dee.....and, er, me.

Yes, there we were.
Oh, what a crowd,
the family clan,
and so, *so* loud!
Shouty and screechy
and yakky and gabby,
and
all gobbling lunch
at Fountains Abbey.

Hide and Seek: the Birthday Game

It was an easy birthday game to play.
I just closed my eyes,
counted to one hundred,
then shouted,
"Ready or not, I'm coming!"
     It was easy.

Or was it?
I searched for my four cousins
right through our house.
"I'll find you!"
But where were they hiding?
     Where?

I searched under beds,
inside wardrobes,
beneath tables.....
Ah, the cupboard
under the stairs.
     But.....no one there.

I looked behind doors,
around the shower curtain,
in the bath,
inside blanket boxes.
Where *were* they?
     Where?

Maybe the cellar?
It was dark and damp

down there,
and a rusty tap drip drip dripped.
What was *that?*
  A *rat?*

They *must* be
in the attic -
so,
I climbed the steep stairs,
pushed open the hatch.
  It creaked..... spookily.

I peered into
cardboard boxes,
an old trunk,
behind a wobbly bookcase
and a cobwebby chest of
  drawers.....

"Is there anyone here?"
Silence.
No one.
I returned
to where I started, and shouted,
  "All right, I give up!"

After a few minutes
they emerged,
one by one by one.
"Where were you?
Where did you hide?
  Where?"

Ben tapped the side of his nose.
"Secret," he said.
The others grinned.
No one was telling.
My four cousins just stood there,
         grinning.

That was on my 10th birthday.
And even today,
many, many years later,
I *still* don't know
where they hid.
         It's a mystery.

         An unsolved mystery.

Winter.....

Guard Wolf in Siberia

My coat is thick,
my teeth are strong,
the snow lies deep,
the winter's long.

I stand on guard
here in the cold.
The pack's asleep.
Some grow old.
I live by hunting.
Men hunt me.
When guns spit fire
I run, I flee.

My coat is thick,
my teeth are strong,
the snow lies deep,
the winter's long.

In fairy tales
I roamed the wood,
the bad wolf in
'Red Riding Hood'.
If I howl now
the pack will wake.
We'll race across
the frozen lake.

My coat is thick,
my teeth are strong,
the snow lies deep,
the winter's long.

Winter's Wolf

Global warming? Not yet, not quite.....
for winter's chilling wolf still prowls
with hackles raised and fur snow-white.
At darkfall he rounds the gable-end
all north wind snarl and freezing bite
      on Christmas night,
      on Christmas night.

Now make the house secure and tight,
throw on more yule logs so they blaze,
sip mulled wine, make the fir tree bright,
ignore the fanged wolf's wintry howls,
and fill each room with golden light
      this Christmas night,
      this Christmas night.

The Harbour Wall

In winter,
when chill winds blow
and the sea is grey-white
as an icy puddle,

the harbour wall
curves its long stone arm
around the fishing boats
bob-bobbing in a huddle.

"I'll keep you safe
from winter's storms,"
the wall seems to say,
and it gives the boats a cuddle.

Wes Magee

A Week of Winter Weather

On Monday icy rains poured down
and flooded drains all over town.

Tuesday's gales bashed elm and ash:
dead branches came down with a crash.

On Wednesday bursts of hail and sleet.
No one walked along our street.

Thursday stood out clear and calm
but the Sun was paler than my arm.

Friday's frost that bit your ears
was cold enough to freeze your tears.

Saturday's sky was ghostly grey:
we skated on the lake today.

Christmas Eve was Sunday......and
snow fell like foam across the land.

A Short Cut after Dark

It's
late.
The night is icy
as we head home
after carol singing,
coins chinking in our collecting tin.
It's *so* cold.
Our fingers feel frost-bitten.
The estate is quiet,
there's no one about.
Snow lies on the pavement.
Far away a dog barks.

It's
late.
We decide to take a short cut
through the school grounds.
So, climb the wall, drop,
and race past the 'No Trespassers' sign,
race past the skeletal trees,
the bushes hunched
like sleeping bears.
Beneath our boots
the crisp snow creaks.
So dark, so dark.

It's
late.
Hearts thumping
we stop, breathless,
at the school building.
We inhale fast
and the freezing air
hurts our lungs.
Listen! An owl hoots.
In the clear sky a million stars
are like silver nails hammered into the hull
of a vast, black ship.

It's
late.
The last lap. Wraith-like we skate
across the playground
and vault the padlocked gate.
At last, we reach our street.
No cars. No people.
Three days before Christmas
and our carols long gone
into the frozen night.
Home. Lights in the hall. Warmth.
It's
late.

Still

Snow,
finer than crushed glass,
falls continuously,
smothering road and roof
until the day shivers
to a Christmas card
       still.

Buried,
the Earth's slowed pulse
weathers this deep
       season.

It's Christmas Time!

Carols drift across the night.

Holly gleams by candlelight.

Roaring fire, a spooky tale.

Ice and snow and wind and hail.

Santa seen in High Street store.

Television..... more and *more.*

Mince pies, turkey, glass of wine.

Acting your own pantomime.

Socks hung up. It's Christmas time!

The Christmas Haiku

A Candle
That feather of flame
melting the window's ice skin
guides us through the night.

New Star
Atop the church spire
one hundred coloured bulbs flash
Christmas news in morse.

Christmas Bells
Urgent, they call us
across fields to a barn where
cows, a donkey stand.

Holly Sprig
Berries like blood drops,
and green leaves that remind us
Spring sleeps beyond the hill.

Robin
As heavy snow falls
he's a red-vested Batman
on the garden fence.

Wes Magee

People.....

The Mysterious 'Portrait of Lady Jane'
(seen at West Dean Mansion, Sussex)

Stand in the Great Hall and view
the *'Portrait of Lady Jane'.*
She sits in a summer garden,
cool and serene in a white dress,
holding a letter in her right hand.
In the background you can see

       the calm lake,
       a beech copse,
       and the blue,
       cloudless
       sky.

Step forward. Look closer.
The letter page is blank.
On the lake a rowing boat drifts, empty.
And *has* Lady Jane seen, as you do now,
that hand waving feebly from the water,
the twisted face in the darkling copse,
       and that faint
       flash of lightning
       scarring the blue,
       cloudless
       sky?

The Chimney Boy's Song

"Inside the chimney, high I climb.
It's dark inside the sooty stack.
I bang my head,
I graze my back,
I lose all sense of passing time.
> Inside the chimney
> high I climb.

"Inside the chimney, high I climb.
Far, far above..... there's a patch of blue
where one white cloud drifts into view.
I stop to rest,
but that's a crime.
> Inside the chimney
> high I climb.

"Inside the chimney, high I climb.
My bare feet slip on crumbling bricks.
I clear rooks' nests,
dead leaves and sticks.
The Master yells, *"Get working, brat!"*
I'm starved.
Sometimes I eat stewed rat.
Soot's in my hair.
I'm tasting grime.
> Inside the chimney
> high I climb."

Tracey's Tree

Last year it was not there,
the sapling with purple leaves
planted in the school grounds with care.
It's Tracey's Tree, my friend who died,
and last year it was not there.

Tracey, the girl with long black hair,
who, out playing one day,
ran across a main road for a dare.
The lorry struck her! Now a tree grows,
and last year it was not there.

Through the classroom window I stare
and watch the sapling sway.
Soon its branches will stand bare.
It wears a forlorn and lonely look,
and last year it was not there.

October's chill is in the air
and cold rain distorts my view.
I feel a sadness that's hard to bear.
The tree blurs, as if I've been crying,
and last year it was not there.

A Football Circle

From the fans' throats
  the raucous roar,
    the raucous roar
      then the goalkeeper's throw,
        the goalkeeper's throw
          then the sweeper's pass,
            the sweeper's pass
              then the fullback's flick,
                the fullback's flick
                  then the midfielder's chip,
                    the midfielder's chip
                      then the winger's run,
                    the winger's run
                    then the whipped-in cross,
                the whipped-in cross
              then the striker's header,
            the striker's header
          then the goalkeeper's miss,
        the goalkeeper's miss
      then the winning goal,
    the winning goal
    then the raucous roar,
  the raucous roar
from the fans' throats.

The Skateboard Boys

Last Saturday, walking the dog,
I passed a pub called 'The Three Lamps',
then stopped opposite the skatepark
where skater boys, on concrete ramps,
were performing daredevil stunts.
Hm. *This* wasn't collecting stamps!

The older ones, in t-shirts, jeans,
made high-speed runs down the steep hill,
did twists, turns, jumps, leaps and kickflips.
Fearless. A demo of sheer skill.
Then they'd stop dead at the ramp top,
casually catching their boards. Brill.

I saw others, the boy learners,
uncertain foot-pushers, young lads
who kept to the concrete levels,
kitted out in brand-new knee pads
and elbow guards, helmets and gloves,
birthday presents from grans, mums and dads.

The skater boys didn't notice us
as we stood watching their skilled show,
an invisible man and his dog.
The whole scene was cool speed and flow,
the skateboards rattling on concrete.
The dog whined. It was time to go.

Places.....

The School Classroom.....
at the Midnight Hour

As
  you
    enter
     the
      school
       classroom
        at
         the
          midnight
           hour.....
darkness engulfs you like a winter cloak,
spiders spin webs in gloomy corners,
the door creaks, clock ticks, blinds rattle,
and a sink tap drip, drip, drip, drip, drips.
Words of warning appear on the SMART Board -

Beware!   Danger!! -

while moonbeams cast spooky shadows across the ceiling.
Homework and pens lie forgotten on tables.
Outside.....a barn owl swoops onto a petrified vole.
From a wall poster, the eyes of Henry VIII glare menacingly
as the spirit of a long, long-gone Headteacher
drifts
  silently
    across
     the
      school
       classroom
        at
         the
          midnight
           hour.....

Wes Magee

At the End of a School Day

It is the end of a school day
   and down the long driveway
come bag-swinging, shouting children.
   Deafened, the sky winces.
      The sun gapes in surprise.

Suddenly, the runners skid to a stop,
   stand still and stare
at a small hedgehog
   curled up on the tarmac
      like an old, frayed cricket ball.

A girl dumps her bag, tiptoes forward
   and gingerly, so gingerly,
carries the creature
   to the safety of a shady hedge.
      Then steps back, watching.

Girl, children, sky and sun
   hold their breath.
There is a silence,
   a moment to remember
      on this warm afternoon in June.

The House on the Hill

It was built years ago
by someone quite manic
and sends those who go there
away in blind panic.
They tell tales of horrors
that can injure or kill,
designed by the madman
who lived on the Hill.

> If you visit
> the House on the Hill for a dare,
> remember my words,
> *"There are dangers.*
> *Beware!"*

The piano's white teeth
when you plonk out a note
will bite off your fingers
then reach for your throat.
The living-room curtains –
long, heavy and black –
will wrap you in cobwebs
if you're slow to step back.

> If you enter
> the House on the Hill for a dare,
> remember my words,
> *"There are dangers.*
> *Beware!"*

The fridge in the kitchen
has a self-closing door.
If it knocks you inside
then you're ice cubes......for sure.
The steps to the cellar
are littered with bones,
and up from the darkness
drift creakings and groans.
>   If you go to
>   the House on the Hill for a dare,
>   remember my words,
>   *"There are dangers.*
>   *Beware!"*

Turn on the hot tap
and the bathroom will flood,
not with gallons of water
but litres of blood.
And the rocking-chair's arms
can squeeze you to death:
it's a waste of time shouting
as you run......out......of......breath.
>   So, don't say you weren't warned,
>   or told to take care,
>   when you went to
>   the House on the Hill
>   ......for a dare.

Ah, yes, all those Forgotten Battles of Long, Long Ago......

*(At the Battle of Hastings, in 1066,
King Harold got an arrow in the eye.
We all know that, but what about those
<u>forgotten</u> battles of long, long ago.....?)*

In **1094**..... at the Bruising Brawl outside Basingstoke,
Baron Bertie Basher
experienced a painful prod
in the posterior.
(Aaaargh!)

In **1108**..... at the Loud Lashing in Letchworth,
Lady Lucinda Lambchop
suffered such a nasty nip
on the tip of her nose.
(Ohhhhh!)

In **1159**..... at the Kicking of Knickers beside Knaresborough,
King Kevin (ol' Klever Kloggs 'imself)
got a big brown boot
up his right royal rump.
(Yeeeooowww!)

In **1213**..... at the Awful Affray beyond Aberdeen,
Archbishop Albert Aardvark
received a terrifyingly torturous tweak
of his tiny toe.
(Eeeeek!)

In **1344**..... at the Calamitous Carve-Up in Carmarthen,
       Count Colin de Cowpatt
       endured a walloping whack
          on his wobbly windpipe.
                (Gggaaarrrggghhh!)

In **1399**..... at the Sensational Scrap south of Swindon,
       Saint Samantha Smellie-Sox
       met with an ever-so-painful elbow
          in the earhole.
             (Ooooouch!)

              And
           finally.....

In **1407**..... at the Petrifying Punch-Up near Peterborough,
       Prince Potty de Paul (the 13th)
       ended-up with a nasty knock on the knee,
       a large lump on his lower lip,
       a terrible tug to the thumb,
       and.....
          a noose around his neck.
             (Aaahhhrrrg.......ggg.......ggg.....!)

          Ah, *yes,*
       all those forgotten battles
          of long,
         long ago..........

Snagger's Pond

Snagger's Pond was dying.
There was bad pollution.
So, what could we do?
What *was* the solution?

We dragged out bicycle tyres,
   rusty wheels, sogged plastic bags,
an old brolly, worn trainers,
   tangled twine and rotting rags.
We pulled out a Wellington boot,
   a headless doll, slimy stones,
handfuls of decaying leaves,
   bats and balls, beanbags and bones.

Then we hosed in water for hours,
   introduced scores of water snails,
aquatic plants, green duckweed,
   frogspawn, and pebbles in pails.
We put in a pair of newts,
   and fish – a dozen or more –
then watched the minnows, ghost carp,
   and small goldfish explore.

Snagger's Pond was dying.
There was bad pollution.
So, we cleaned and restocked.
We *found* the solution.

The Travelling Britain Rap

All the drivers
rattling on
in a million
fast cars
driving up
and down
the country
like motor racing stars,
on clearway
    motorway
        carriageway
            and street
then roundabout
and road
through rain
    and hail
        and sleet
driving up
and down
the country
till they're feeling
dead beat
and the
    traffic noise
        traffic noise
            has turned
            them
                half
                    deaf

so they take
a welcome break
at Deeno's Diner,
Little Chef

and

(guzzle,
guzzle,
gulp,
gulp)

then

(gasp.....gasp.....)

they're

driving on
driving on
as the tyres
zip and zap
through a thousand
towns and cities
that are dotted
on the map
at *least*
a million cars
overtaking
through
that
gap

never stopping
   city hopping
never stopping
   city hopping
never stopping
   city hopping
for all the cars
are moving
to the travelling
Britain rap
for all the cars
are moving
to the travelling
Britain rap
for all the cars
are moving
to the

    travelling

      Britain

        rap

Sweeeeeeeeeesh!

You've reached the end.....

Well read,
  well done,
    you've reached
      the end.

Hope you
  enjoyed
    the book,
      my friend.

Best wishes
  and congrats
    from
      me,

the poet-
  author,
    Wes
      Magee.

(Page 56 answer: 55 children started the cross country race)